# IT TAKES A VILLAGE

## BY: BERNETTA W. FARMER

LIFE'S GOLDEN TRINKETS PUBLICATIONS

BACK IN THE DAY

WHEN GREAT GRANDMA WAS ALIVE.

CERTAIN VALUES WERE TAUGHT

WHEN MY MOTHER WAS A CHILD.

VALUES WERE PASSED DOWN

TO MY MOTHER TO THIS DAY.

A CHILD SHOULD STAY

IN A CHILD'S PLACE SHE'D SAY.

CORE VALUES WERE BUILT

AND STAYED AS I GREW OLDER.

IT KEPT ME GROUNDED AND FOCUSED

WHICH ALLOWED ME TO GROW STRONGER.

SNEAKING TO LISTEN

AS ELDERS GATHERED TOGETHER TO TALK.

THEY WOULD SAY WITH A FIRM WORD,

"STAY OUT OF GROWN FOLKS MOUTH."

WE KNEW WHEN TO SPEAK.

WE KNEW WHEN TO LISTEN.

FOR IF WE DIDN'T

A STRONG WORD WOULD GRAB OUR ATTENTION.

THE COMMUNITY USED TO BE SAFER.

OUR DOORS DIDN'T HAVE TO BE SECURED.

TIMES HAVE CHANGED ALL AROUND US

REGARDING THE LIVES OF OUR YOUTH.


THERE USED TO BE A TIME

IF THINGS GOT OUT OF HAND

PARENTS MAYBE LATE FROM WORK

THE VILLAGE WOULD TAKE A STAND.

When the street lights would come on
around 5:00 or 6 o'clock
the village came together and made sure we
were inside the house.

YOU'RE NOT SUPPOSED TO BE OUT THIS LATE.

WE'LL CALL YOUR PARENTS THEY'D SAY.

WE WOULD HURRY TO GET HOME AND NOT MAKE HASTE.

NO STOPPING BY A FRIEND'S

OR THE STORE TO GET SOME TREATS.

STRAIGHT HOME IS WHERE WE WOULD GO.

A SAFE PLACE FOR US TO BE.

HARD TIMES HAS A WAY

OF QUICKLY CHANGING THINGS.

BABIES HAVING BABIES AND NOT THINKING.

THESE TYPE OF DECISIONS IN LIFE IT SEEMS

WILL POST PONE ALL OF THEIR VALUABLE DREAMS.

GIVING THEMSELVES TO YOUNG MEN

WITH FALSE PROMISES.

QUICK WITH THEIR SMOOTH TALKS

AND NOT EQUIPPED TO BECOME A FATHER YET.

YOUNG CHILDREN ARE NOT READY

TO BECOME PARENTS TOO SOON.

LEARN TO WAIT.  THE TIME MUST BE RIGHT.

THEY'LL APPRECIATE IT LATER, IT'S TRUE.

WHERE ARE THE VILLAGES THAT ARE NEEDED TODAY?

BECOMING A POSITIVE EXAMPLE

IN SHOWING YOUTH A BETTER WAY.

THERE ARE STILL SOME VILLAGES

THAT KEEP THE COMMUNITES STRONG.

TAKE AN INTEREST IN YOUR COMMUNITY

AND PASS THIS KNOWLEDGE ALONG.

BE A POSITIVE ROLE MODEL

IT'S THE ONE THING THAT WILL WIN IT.

TO KEEP THEIR FUTURE ON THE RISE

TO RAISE A CHILD IT TAKES A VILLAGE.

DANGER AWAITS PATIENTLY.

WHEN A CHILD'S OUT RUNNING THE STREETS.

THE VILLAGE MUST BE CONCERNED

FOR THEIR SAFETY IS THE KEY.

WITH LOVE SET A STRONG FOUNDATION

POSITIVE, FIRM WORDS TO SEND THEM HOME WITH.

REMEMBER IN THESE DIFFERENT TIMES

TO RAISE A CHILD IT TAKES A VILLAGE.

VILLAGE COMMUNITY LET'S GET BACK
TO THE EXAMPLE WE USED TO BE.
BECOMING A POSITIVE ROLE MODEL
A VERY IMPORTANT PIECE.

BE CAREFUL HOW YOU REACT AROUND A CHILD.

THEIR MINDS ARE LIKE A SPONGE.

ABSORBING EVERY MOVE YOU MAKE.

ESPECIALLY THE NEGATIVE ONES.

BEING AROUND THE WRONG CROWD

NOT A GOOD PLACE TO BE.

SOMETIMES THE CHILD WILL IGNORE

WARNING SIGNS THAT THEIR PARENT'S SPEAK.

DANGER IS ON THE PROWL CHILDREN

AND IT DOESN'T CARE WHO YOU ARE.

LET THE VILLAGE TEACH YOU TO BE SAFE

FOR YOU ARE SOMEBODY'S CHILD.

PLEASE TAKE HEED TO THE LESSONS.

THINGS ARE VERY DIFFERENT NOW.

BE CAREFUL WHEN CHOOSING FRIENDS.

IT TAKES A VILLAGE TO RAISE A CHILD.

IT TAKES A VILLAGE TO RAISE A CHILD.

OF COURSE ONE MIGHT SAY.

BUT NO ONE WANTS TO TAKE THE LEAD.

TOO BUSY OR TOO AFRAID.

A POSITIVE ROLE MODEL IS NEEDED

TO SHOW THEM THE ROPES.

KEEPING THEM AWAY FROM DRUGS

AND BUILDING UP THEIR HOPES.

A BUILDING BLOCK OF STRENGTH

ONE DAY AT A TIME.

WE NEED TO BUILD ONE ANOTHER

TO FORM A VILLAGE AND HELP A CHILD.

CHILDREN HURTING CHILDREN

NOT THE WAY FOR THEIR FUTURE TO BE BRIGHTER.

THE JOURNEY IS MUCH GREATER FOR THEM.

LET'S MAKE THEIR LOAD A LITTLE LIGHTER.


WHAT HAPPENS WHEN THE COMMUNITY

COMES TOGETHER TO MAKE A CHANGE.

LESS VIOLENCE OCCURS, FEWER DRUGS ARE CONSUMED

AND THE WORLD IS A BETTER PLACE.

NOT BEING TAUGHT THE VALUE OF LIFE.

HELPING THEM TO CHOOSE THE RIGHT ROAD.

BECOMING A GUIDING LIGHT TO THEM.

HELP THEM REACH THEIR LIFE'S GOAL.

THE VILLAGE MUST EDUCATE OUR CHILDREN.

LET'S GET THEM BACK TO BEING PROUD

OF WHO THEY ARE AND WHAT THEY STAND FOR.

IT TAKES A VILLAGE TO RAISE A CHILD.

GUIDE THEM IN BEING GRATEFUL

FOR THE THINGS THAT THEY HAVE.

IN A HURRY TO WANT MATERIAL THINGS

WILL MAKE THEM TAKE WHAT IS NOT THEIRS.

TEACH THEM NOT TO TAKE FOR GRANTED

THE LIFE THAT'S BEEN GIVEN TO THEM.

FOR IT TAKES A VILLAGE TO SHOW THEM THE WAY

SO THEY CAN HAVE A SECOND CHANCE.

BEGIN TO REACH OUT TO A CHILD.

IT TAKES ONE DAY A TIME.

LET THEM KNOW HOW IMPORTANT THEY ARE.

FOR IT TAKES A VILLAGE TO RAISE A CHILD.

STRONG LEADERS CAN BE BIRTHED.

POSITIVES CHANGES CAN STRETCH WIDE.

TEACH THEM HOW TO SURVIVE IN LIFE

AND KEEP THEIR DREAMS ALIVE.

WITH A STRONG AND POSITIVE FOUNDATION

TO GUIDE THEM TOWARD DESTINY.

A VITAL PIECE OF INFORMATION

TO PREPARE THEM FOR THEIR DREAM.

A VILLAGE CAN LEAD THE CHILDREN

IN THE RIGHT DIRECTION.

LOOKING OUT FOR THEIR BEHALF

TOGETHER WITH THE GUIDANCE OF THE PARENTS.

LET'S SHOW THEM THE STRONG VILLAGE
THAT USED TO BE BACK IN THE DAY.
SPREADING HOPE AND CARE THEY LONG FOR
FOR IT'S THE AMERICAN WAY.

BRINGING ABOUT A POSITIVE CHANGE.

SHOW THEM THAT WE CARE.

THEY WILL LEARN TO REACH OUT TO OTHERS

WITH THIS POSITIVE ATMOSPHERE.

WHEN WE BEGIN TO COME TOGETHER.

THEY TOO WILL GET INVOLVED.

THEY DESERVE TO HAVE A FUTURE.

IT TAKES A VILLAGE TO RAISE A CHILD.

LET'S STOP FIGHTING AMONGST OURSELVES

AND BECOME THE POSITIVE MENTOR.

IF WE CANNOT COME TOGETHER

THEIR FUTURE CAN BE LOST FOREVER.

SO CALLING ALL LEADERS AND MENTORS

TO LEND A HELPING HAND.

FOR WE DON'T' WANT OUR CHILDREN

LOST IN A WORLD THAT'S NEGATIVE.

A CHILD NEEDS GUIDANCE AND HOPE TO BE POSITIVE.

REMEMBER THEY DESERVE A FUTURE.

TO RAISE A CHILD IT TAKES A VILLAGE.

# LIFE IS WORTH LIVING

# IT TAKES A VILLAGE

Published by: Life's Golden Trinkets Publications
All rights reserved. Unauthorized duplication is in violation of applicable laws.
TM and copyright by Bernetta W, Farmer, Life's Golden Trinkets Publications © 2016
Copyright © 2016

Life's Golden Trinkets Publications
7399 Shadeland Ave .STE #137
Indianapolis, IN 46250

IT TAKES A VILLAGE
ISBN 978-0-9893245-3-3

www.ingramcontent.com/pod-product-compliance
Lightning Source LLC
Chambersburg PA
CBHW042116040426
42449CB00002B/69